Lynne Rowe was taught to knit and crochet by her grandmother in her early childhood and has been hooked ever since. She has developed a wide range of specialist skills and love to pass these on to others through her workshops and classes. She is best known for her whimsical designs which feature regularly in the UK's most popular craft magazines, along with articles and technical guides. Her practical approach makes her patterns straightforward, easy to read and fun to make. Her aim is to encourage as many other people as possible to knit and crochet.

Lynne is well-known in the crochet community, and her books have sold over 85k copies worldwide. See more of her work on her website www.knitcrochetcreate.com and @knitcrochetcreate on Instagram. Lynne lives in Congleton, Cheshire, UK.

Like this book? Here are some more in this series:

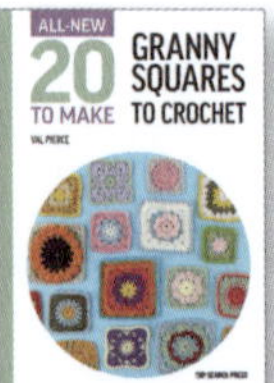

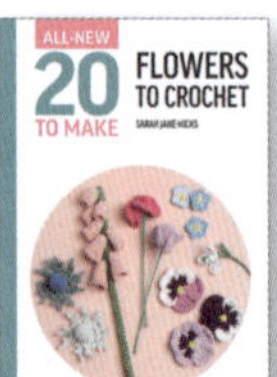

9781800921467   9781800921399   9781800921009   9781800922181

To discover the full range of titles in the *All-New 20 to Make* series, scan the QR code, right or visit www.searchpress.com

20 TO MAKE

CROCHET DISHCLOTHS

Lynne Rowe

SEARCH PRESS

First published in 2026

Search Press Limited
Wellwood, North Farm Road,
Tunbridge Wells, Kent TN2 3DR

1 2 3 4 5 6 7 8 9 10

Text copyright © Lynne Rowe 2026
Photographs by Stacy Grant
Photographs and design copyright © Search Press Ltd. 2026

ISBN: 978-1-80092-356-0
ebook ISBN: 978-1-80093-339-2

Bookmarked Hub

For further ideas and inspiration, and to join our free online community, visit www.bookmarkedhub.com

Publishers' notes

Imperial measurements are used in this book; the metric conversions are rounded to the nearest 0.5cm. Always use either metric or imperial measurements, not a combination of both.

US crochet terms are used throughout this book. For UK equivalents please refer to page 10.

The Publishers and author can accept no responsibility for any consequences arising from the information, advice or instructions given in this publication.

For errata, please visit our website (www.searchpress.com) or the Bookmarked Hub (www.bookmarkedhub.com).

GPSR information can be found at www.searchpress.com

Printed in China, AP032025

INTRODUCTION

There are so many things to love about crochet dishcloths, and they're one of my favourite quick makes – my go-to project when I'm not sure what to make next.

They're simple, satisfying and practical, but most of all, I love them because they're the perfect projects for using up leftover yarn from your stash. Whether it's those odd 50g balls of cotton yarn or small scraps of different colours, they're all ideal for crocheting colourful and creative dishcloths.

Dishcloths are a great way to practise new stitches, and they also make wonderful handmade gifts – especially when wrapped up with a handmade soap, a candle or a small kitchen accessory. They're small, thoughtful and practical – perfect for friends, neighbours or anyone who loves something handmade.

Each design in this book is easy to pick up and put down, with clear instructions and simple stitches that create beautiful textures. Whether you're making them for your own kitchen or as thoughtful gifts, these dishcloths are a lovely way to enjoy a few minutes of mindful crochet.

With twenty different designs to choose from, you can try new stitch patterns, play with colour and make something useful at the same time.

So grab your yarn, pick a pattern and let's get crocheting!

Lynne

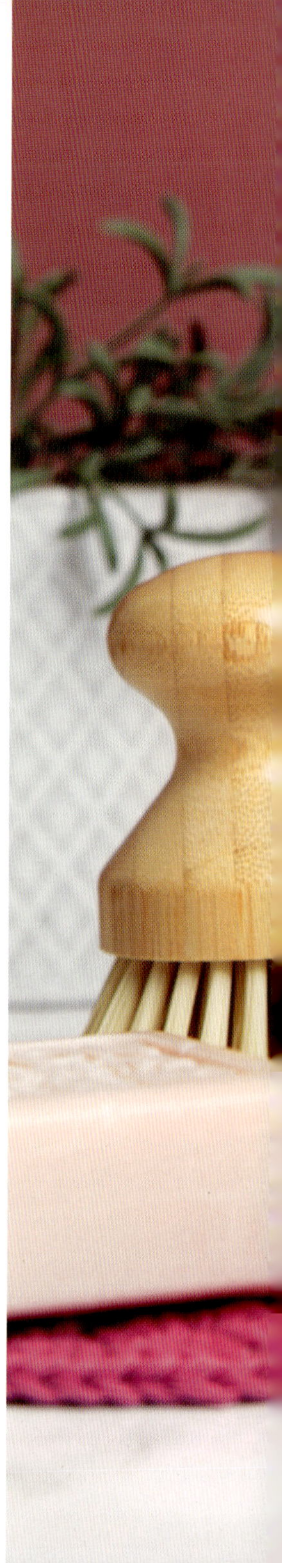

TOOLS & MATERIALS

You only need a few basic items to crochet your own dishcloths,
which makes it so simple to get started!

CROCHET HOOKS

The patterns in the book use the following hook sizes:

- 2.5mm (UK 12, US C/2)
- 3mm (UK 11, US D/3)
- 3.5mm (UK 9, US E/4)
- 4mm (UK 8, US G/6)
- 4.5mm (UK 7, US 7)
- 5mm (UK 6, US H/8)

OTHER TOOLS

SCISSORS

Use a small sharp pair of scissors for snipping threads.

WOOL/TAPESTRY NEEDLE

Thread your yarn onto a wool or tapestry needle when darning
in ends.

TAPE MEASURE

Use a flexible tape measure to check your gauge (tension).

STITCH MARKERS

Stitch markers can be useful for marking a particular stitch in
a row.

BLOCKING EQUIPMENT, OPTIONAL:

If you prefer to block your dishcloths to keep them looking neat,
I'd recommend using the following:

- Spray water bottle or a hand-held clothes steamer
- Rust-proof pins
- Foam mats or towel.

YARN

Dishcloths are best made with cotton yarn, as it's absorbent, durable and washes well. Depending on the pattern, you can choose from the following yarn weights:

- Yarn weight 2: sport weight/fingering (4-ply)
- Yarn weight 3: light worsted/8-ply (double knitting)
- Yarn weight 4: worsted/10-ply (Aran).

Cotton blends with linen or bamboo can also work nicely for a softer or slightly textured finish.

Avoid acrylic yarns or wool, as they don't absorb water as well and may not dry quickly, so while the patterns will look similar, they won't make very practical dishcloths.

If you're using up yarn from your stash, check that it's smooth and non-stretchy because these fibres hold their shape and show off stitch details beautifully.

Natural fibres like cotton are also biodegradable and long-lasting, making them a sustainable and eco-friendly choice for everyday use.

TIP: Always wash your finished dishcloths before use to remove any residue from the yarn.

ABBREVIATIONS

Note: all patterns in this book use US crochet terms.

US ABBREVIATION	US	UK
beg	begin/beginning	begin/beginning
BLO	back loop only	back loop only
BPdc	back post double crochet	back post treble crochet (BPtr)
ch	chain	chain
dc	double crochet	treble crochet (tr)
FLO	front loop only	front loop only
FPdc	front post double crochet	front post treble crochet (FPtr)
hdc	half double crochet	half treble crochet (htr)
pm	place marker	place marker
rep	repeat	repeat
RS	right side	right side
sc	single crochet	double crochet (dc)
sc2tog	single crochet 2 stitches together (to decrease 1 st)	double crochet 2 stitches together (dc2tog) (to decrease 1 st)
sc3tog	single crochet 3 stitches together (to decrease 2 sts)	double crochet 3 stitches together (dc3tog) (to decrease 2 sts)
skip	skip	miss
sl st	slip stitch	slip stitch
sp	space	space
st	stitches	stitches
tr	treble crochet	double treble crochet (dtr)
tr2tog	treble crochet 2 stitches together (to decrease 1 st)	double treble crochet 2 stitches together (dtr2tog) (to decrease 1 st)
tr3tog	treble crochet 3 stitches together (to decrease 2 sts)	double treble crochet 3 stitches together (dtr3tog) (to decrease 2 sts)
WS	wrong side	wrong side
yrh	yarn round hook	yarn round hook

TECHNIQUES

The following special stitches are used in some of the patterns in this book. Each one adds variety and texture to your dishcloths, and you can refer back to these instructions whenever needed.

SPECIAL STITCHES

3 double crochet cluster (3dc-Cl)
*yrh, insert hook into stitch, yrh and pull a loop through, yrh and pull through first 2 loops only; rep from * twice more in same st (4 loops on hook), yrh and pull through all 4 loops.

Bobble stitch (bobble)
*yrh, insert hook into st, yrh and pull a loop through, yrh and pull through first 2 loops only; rep from * twice more in same st (4 loops on hook), yrh and pull through all 4 loops. Where the next st is a sc, the bobble will be raised on RS of work.

Corner-to-corner crochet (C2C crochet)
Each row is made by creating a series of 'blocks' that consist of (3 ch and 3 dc). On each row, one extra block is worked at the beginning of a row to increase, then one block fewer is worked to decrease.

Picot stitch (picot)
3 ch, sl st in second ch from hook, sl st in next ch.

Popcorn stitch (popcorn st)
4 dc in stitch as specified in pattern, remove hook from working loop, insert hook in top of first dc from front to back, replace working loop on hook and pull through.

Puff stitch (puff st)
*yrh, insert hook into st, yrh and pull a loop through, rep from * twice more in same st (7 loops on hook), yrh and pull through all 7 loops.

V-stitch (V-st)
(1 dc, 1 ch, 1 dc) into same stitch or space.

HANGING LOOP

16 chain (or a chain as long as desired), sl st into same st or sp, sl st into each ch around the loop, sl st in first sl st. Fasten off and weave in ends.

HINTS & TIPS

Crochet dishcloths are quick and satisfying to make. They're perfect
for using up small amounts of yarn, trying new stitches and creating
something useful for your home, as well as helping to reduce single-use
or disposable household cloths and scourers. They also make thoughtful,
eco-friendly gifts.

Below are a few handy hints to bear in mind when making and using your
crochet dishcloths.

GAUGE (TENSION)

Dishcloths don't need to fit a specific size, so tension isn't critical.
However, if your stitches are very loose, the cloth may stretch more in
use. If you prefer a firmer finish, use a hook one size smaller.

DISHCLOTHS DON'T HAVE TO BE SQUARE!

Experiment with different shapes and sizes depending on what you'll
use them for. Rectangular cloths work well for cleaning surfaces,
while round or hexagonal ones make lovely gifts or decorative pieces.
Small squares are great for testing out new stitch patterns.

*Textured stitches make great scourers
that won't scatch your pots and
pans. See page 21 to make the
Flower Scrubbie on the right.*

Liven up your cleaning routine with the cheery and practical Bobble Stripes dishcloth (see page 30).

Dishcloths are relaxing projects to crochet, perfect for taking a little time to yourself. Find the Corner Granny pattern on page 44.

WASHING AND CARING FOR YOUR CROCHET DISHCLOTHS

Machine wash or hand wash your dishcloths regularly to keep them clean and fresh. Most cotton yarns can be washed at 100°F (40°C). Reshape and dry flat to keep them neat. A quick iron on a low setting helps smooth them out, if needed.

STAIN REMOVING

For stubborn stains, soak your dishcloths in warm water with a little mild detergent or baking soda before washing. Avoid products containing bleach, as they can weaken natural fibres and fade colours over time.

FOLLOW THE YARN LABEL LAUNDRY INSTRUCTIONS

Always check the yarn label for specific care details. Some cotton blends or coloured yarns may have lower recommended washing temperatures or need gentle cycles to prevent fading.

DO DISHCLOTHS NEED TO BE WASHED SEPARATELY FROM THE REST OF YOUR LAUNDRY?

No – cotton dishcloths can usually be washed with your regular household laundry. Just avoid mixing them with items that may catch on the stitches, such as anything with zips or hooks.

THE DISHCLOTHS

CORNER-TO-CORNER

The classic Corner-to-Corner (C2C) stitch gives this dishcloth a block-like texture that's both sturdy and stylish. Worked diagonally from one corner to the opposite corner, it's a fun and satisfying project that grows quickly and creates a tidy square shape.

SIZE

Approximately 9½in (24cm) square

YOU WILL NEED

- 1 x 137yd/125m/1¾oz/50g ball of sport/ fingering (4-ply) weight cotton yarn in fuchsia pink (A). Shown in Scheepjes Catona 50g (125m) in Garden Rose 251 (A)

- 3.5mm (UK 9, US E/4) crochet hook

TENSION/GAUGE

Not critical, but as a guide, 7.5 x 7.5 C2C blocks measure 4 x 4in (10 x 10cm) using Scheepjes Catona and 3.5mm (UK 9, US E/4) hook

SPECIAL TECHNIQUE

C2C crochet (see page 12 for details)

INSTRUCTIONS

Using yarn A, make a slipknot onto hook.

Row 1 (RS): 6 ch, 1 dc in fourth ch from hook, 1 dc in each of next 2 ch, turn (1 block made).

Row 2 (inc row): 6 ch, 1 dc in fourth ch from hook, 1 dc in each of next 2 ch (1 block made), skip next 3 sts, sl st into sp before 3-ch at end of next block, 3 ch, 3 dc into same sp (1 block made), turn (you now have 2 blocks in total on this row).

Row 3 (inc row): 6 ch, 1 dc in fourth ch from hook, 1 dc in each of next 2 ch (1 block made), *skip next 3 sts, sl st into sp before 3-ch at end of next block, 3 ch, 3 dc into same sp (1 block made), rep from * to end, turn (you now have 3 blocks in total on this row).

Rep row 3 fourteen more times (you have 17 blocks on the last row), ending with WS facing for next row.

Next row (dec row): sl st into each of next 3 sts, *sl st into sp before 3-ch at end of block, (3 ch, 3 dc) into same 3-ch sp (1 block made), rep from * until 1 block remains, sl st into sp before 3-ch at end of last block, turn (16 blocks).

Rep last row until you have worked final row (1 block). At end of row, turn, sl st into each of next 3 sts, sl st into sp before 3-ch at end of block, turn. RS is now facing. Do not fasten off.

BORDER

Some blocks are upright with the tops of the 3 dc along the edge, and alternate blocks are sideways with the post of the dc along the edge.

PATTERN NOTE: When working the border, for upright blocks of 3 dc groups, work (1 sc, 1 ch) in first st, skip next st, work (1 sc, 1 ch) in next st, and in sideways blocks work (1 sc into post of st, 1 ch).

Round 1 (RS): 1 ch (does not count as st), (1 sc, 1 ch, 1 sc, 1 ch) into same sp for corner, work (1 sc, 1 ch) to next corner as instructed in pattern note, rep all around with (1 sc, 1 ch, 1 sc, 1 ch) into each corner, and (1 sc, 1 ch) as instructed above to next corner, sl st in first st, sl st into 2-ch corner sp (110 sts).

If desired, work a 16-ch loop (see 'Hanging Loop', page 12).

Fasten off and weave in ends on WS.

FLOWER SCRUBBIES

These pretty flower-shaped pads are as practical as they are decorative. Each has a textured centre made with loop stitch, perfect for tackling tougher kitchen messes. Made in two colours, they're a cheerful, reusable alternative to disposable scrubbers.

SIZE

Approximately 6in (15cm) across

YOU WILL NEED

- 1 x 137yd/125m/1¾oz/50g ball of 10-ply/worsted (Aran) weight cotton in each of cream and light jade. Shown in Yarn and Colors Epic 50g (85m) in Cream 002 (A) and Jade Gravel 073 (B)

- 5mm (UK 6, US H/8) crochet hook

- Stitch marker

TENSION/GAUGE

Not critical for this project

PATTERN NOTES

The centre circle is worked in back loops only.

Picot stitch is worked into the spare front loops of the centre stitches, to create a textured centre.

SPECIAL STITCHES

Picot stitch (see page 12 for details)

INSTRUCTIONS

CENTRE

Using yarn A, make a magic ring.

Round 1 (RS): 1 ch (does not count as st), 7 sc into ring (7 sts).

Pm in last st of round and move it up as you work.

Round 2: 2 sc in BLO of each st around (14 sts).

Round 3: *1 sc in BLO of next st, 2 sc in BLO of next st, rep from * six more times (21 sts).

Round 4: *1 sc in BLO of next 2 sts, 2 sc in BLO of next st, rep from * six more times (28 sts).

Round 5: *1 sc in BLO of next 3 sts, 2 sc in BLO of next st, rep from * six more times (35 sts). Fasten off.

With RS facing, rejoin yarn A to spare (front) loop of first st of round 1, *1 picot, sl st in FLO of next st along, rep from * to end of round 4 (70 picots).

Fasten off and weave in ends on WS.

PETALS

Using yarn B and with RS facing, join yarn with sl st to any st of round 5.

Round 1 (RS): 1 ch (does not count as st here and throughout), *1 sc in next 2 sts, 1 hdc in next st, 3 dc in next st, 1 hdc in next st, 1 sc in next 2 sts, rep from * four more times, sl st in first sc to join (5 petals) (45 sts).

Round 2: 1 ch, *1 sc in next 2 sts, 1 hdc in next 2 sts, 3 dc in next st, 1 hdc in next 2 sts, 1 sc in next 2 sts, rep from * four more times, sl st in first st (55 sts).

Round 3: 1 ch, *1 sc in next 2 sts, 1 hdc in next 3 sts, 3 dc in next st, 1 hdc in next 3 sts, 1 sc in next 2 sts, rep from * four more times, sl st in first st (65 sts).

Round 4: *sl st in next 2 sts, 1 sc in next 3 sts, 2 sc in next st, 1 dc in next st, 2 sc in next st, 1 sc in next 3 sts, sl st in next 2 sts, rep from * four more times, sl st in first sl st to join (75 sts).

Fasten off and weave in ends on WS.

Make another scrubbie using colours as above, and a third scrubbie using yarn B for the centre and yarn A for the petals.

MOSS STITCH

Using a simple and effective combination of single crochet
and chain stitches, you can create a soft, woven texture. Made in
neat blocks of grey, pale blue and white, this dishcloth has a clean,
modern look that fits beautifully into any kitchen.

SIZE

Approximately 9½in (24cm) square

YOU WILL NEED

- 1 x 64yd/58m/¾oz/25g ball of 8-ply/light
  worsted (DK) weight cotton yarn in each of
  grey (A), pale blue (B) and off-white (C). Shown
  in Ricorumi DK 25g (58m) in Pearl Grey 004 (A),
  Light Blue 033 (B) and Cream 002 (C)

- 4mm (UK 8, US G/6) crochet hook

TENSION/GAUGE

Not critical, but as a guide, 24 sts and 24 rows
in pattern measure 4 x 4in (10 x 10cm) using
Ricorumi DK and 4mm (UK 8, US G/6) hook

PATTERN NOTES

There is no beginning chain at the start of each
row, creating a much straighter edge with
this stitch pattern.

Chain sts are included in the stitch counts.

INSTRUCTIONS

Using yarn A, 58 ch.

Row 1 (RS): 1 sc in second ch from hook, *1 ch, skip 1 ch, 1 sc
in next ch, rep from * to end, turn (57 sts).

Row 2: 1 sc in first st, 1 sc in next 1-ch sp, *1 ch, skip next st,
1 sc in next 1-ch sp, rep from * to last sc, 1 sc in last st, turn.

Row 3: 1 sc in first st, *1 ch, skip next st, 1 sc in next 1-ch sp,
rep from * to last 2 sts, 1 ch, skip next st, 1 sc in last st, turn.

Rows 4–18: rep rows 2 and 3 seven more times, then rep row
2; change to yarn B on last yrh of last st.

Rows 19–36: using yarn B, rep row 3, then rep rows 2 and 3
eight more times, then rep row 2; change to yarn C on last yrh
of last st.

Rows 37–54: using yarn C, rep row 3, then rep rows 2 and 3
eight more times, then rep row 2, turn.

Row 55: 1 sc in each st and each 1-ch sp to end.

If desired, work a hanging loop (see 'Hanging Loop', page 12).

Fasten off and weave in ends on WS.

"""

V-STITCH

The classic V-stitch gives this dishcloth a light and lacy feel while still being practical for everyday use. Crocheted in a variegated yarn of greens and blues, the colours flow gently together creating a calm and fresh feel.

SIZE

Approximately 9in (23cm) square

YOU WILL NEED

▸ 1 x 130yd/119m/1¾oz/50g ball of 8-ply/light worsted (DK) weight cotton in variegated green/blue. Shown in Nikkim Vinnis Colours 50g (119m) in Green Mix 10 (A)

▸ 4mm (UK 8, US G/6) crochet hook

TENSION/GAUGE

Not critical, but as a guide, 7.5 V-sts and 10 rows in pattern measure 4 x 4in (10 x 10cm) using Vinnis Colours and 4mm (UK 8, US G/6) hook

PATTERN NOTES

Half double crochet stitches are used at the beginning and end of rows, creating a much straighter edge with this stitch pattern.

SPECIAL STITCHES

V-stitch (see page 12 for details)

INSTRUCTIONS

Using yarn A, 38 ch.

Row 1 (RS): (1 dc, 1 ch, 1 dc) in fourth ch from hook (skipped 3 ch counts as 1 hdc, skip 1 ch), *skip 1 ch, (1 dc, 1 ch, 1 dc) in next ch, rep from * to last 2 ch, skip 1 ch, 1 hdc in last ch, turn (17 V-sts, 2 hdc).

Row 2: 2 ch (counts as 1 hdc), *(1 dc, 1 ch, 1 dc) in 1-ch sp of next V-st, rep from * to last st, 1 hdc in last st, turn.

Row 2 sets pattern.

Rows 3–23: rep row 2 twenty-one more times (or until dishcloth is square).

If desired, work a 16-ch loop (see 'Hanging Loop', page 12).

Fasten off and weave in ends on WS.

CORAL TEXTURE

Featuring a beautifully textured stitch, this dishcloth is made by working single and double crochets into chain spaces to create a soft but dense fabric that's great for doing the dishes. The colour palette blends bright coral with a soft peach — a warm, sunset-inspired combination to brighten your kitchen.

SIZE

Approximately 9in (23cm) square

YOU WILL NEED

- 1 x 137yd/125m/1¾oz/50g ball of sport/fingering (4-ply) weight cotton yarn in each of coral (A) and peach (B). Shown in Scheepjes Catona Cotton 50g (125m) in Watermelon 252 (A) and Light Coral 264 (B)

- 3.5mm (UK 9, US E/4) crochet hook

TENSION/GAUGE

Not critical, but as a guide, approximately 23 sts and 21 rows in pattern measure 4 x 4in (10 x 10cm) using Scheepjes Catona and 3.5mm (UK 9, US E/4) hook

INSTRUCTIONS

Using yarn A, 54 ch.

Row 1 (RS): 1 sc in second ch from hook, 1 sc in each ch to end, turn (53 sts).

Row 2 (WS): 1 ch (does not count as st here and throughout), 1 sc in first st, *1 ch, skip next st, 1 sc in next st, rep from * to end, turn (27 sts and 26 1-ch sp).

Row 3: 1 ch, 1 sc in first st, *1 dc in next 1-ch sp, 1 sc in next st, rep from * to end, turn.

Rows 2 and 3 set pattern.

Rep rows 2 and 3 seventeen more times; change to yarn B on last yrh of last st.

Using yarn B, rep rows 2 and 3 five more times, then rep row 2 once.

Last row: 1 ch, 1 sc in each st and each 1-ch sp to end.

If desired, work a 16-ch loop (see 'Hanging Loop', page 12).

Fasten off and weave in ends on WS.

TIP: This textured stitch looks great in any colour combination, making it ideal for using up leftover cotton yarns. Blend sandy neutrals or soft sky blues from your stash for a fresh, coastal look.

BOBBLE STRIPES

Bold and fun, this dishcloth uses bobble stitches to create a raised texture every sixth row, adding extra scrubbing power. Worked in cheerful shades of yellow and mustard, it brings a sunny, retro vibe to your kitchen while still being tough enough for daily use.

SIZE

Approximately 8¾in (22cm) square

YOU WILL NEED

- 1 x 27yd/25m/¼oz/10g ball of sport/fingering (4-ply) weight cotton yarn in each of pale yellow (A), bright yellow (B) and mustard (C). Shown in Scheepjes Catona Cotton 10g (25m) in Primrose 522 (A), Yellow Gold 208 (B) and Saffron 249 (C)

- 3.5mm (UK 9, US E/4) crochet hook

TENSION/GAUGE

Not critical, but as a guide, approximately 23 sts and 26 rows in pattern measure 4 x 4in (10 x 10cm) using Scheepjes Catona and 3.5mm (UK 9, US E/4) hook

SPECIAL STITCHES

Bobble stitch (see page 12 for details)

INSTRUCTIONS

Using yarn A, 52 ch.

Row 1 (RS): 1 sc in second ch from hook, 1 sc in each ch to end, turn (51 sts).

Row 2: 1 ch (does not count as st here and throughout), 1 sc in each st to end, turn.

Rows 3–5: as row 2; rep three times.

Row 6 (WS): 1 ch, 1 sc in first 3 sts, *1 bobble in next st, 1 sc in next 3 sts, rep from * to end; change to yarn B on last yrh of last sc, turn (12 bobbles and 39 sc).

Rows 7–11: using yarn B, 1 ch, 1 sc in each st to end, turn.

Row 12: as row 6; change to yarn C on last yrh of last sc, turn.

Rows 7 to 12 set 6-row pattern.

Rows 13–54: rep rows 7–12 seven more times, working each 6-row pattern rep in following colour sequence: C, A, B, C, A, B, C; change to yarn A on last yrh of last sc.

Using yarn A, rep row 2 five more times.

If desired, work a 16-ch loop (see 'Hanging Loop', page 12).

Fasten off and weave in ends on WS.

GREEN GRANNY

This dishcloth puts a twist on the classic granny square, starting with an open centre and moving into solid rounds for extra durability. Made in two shades of green to give a fresh feel that's perfect for a handmade touch in the kitchen.

SIZE

Approximately 9in (23cm) square

YOU WILL NEED

- 1 x 130yd/119m/1¾oz/50g ball of 8-ply/light worsted (DK) weight cotton yarn in each of pale green (A) and mid green (B). Shown in Nikkim Vinnis Colours 50g (119m) in Apple Green 553 (A) and Fern 529 (B)

- 4mm (UK 8, US G/6) crochet hook

TENSION/GAUGE

Not critical, but as a guide, first 6 rounds of pattern measure approximately 4 x 4in (10 x 10cm) using Vinnis Colours and 4mm (UK 8, US G/6) hook

INSTRUCTIONS

Using yarn A, make a magic ring.

Round 1 (RS): 3 ch (counts as 1 dc throughout), 2 dc in ring, 2 ch, (3 dc in ring, 2 ch) three times, sl st in top of beg 3-ch (12 sts, 4 corner 2-ch sp).

Round 2: sl st in each of next 2 sts, sl st into corner sp, 3 ch, (2 dc, 2 ch, 3 dc) in same corner sp, *(3 dc, 2 ch, 3 dc) in next corner sp, rep from * twice more, sl st in top of beg 3-ch (24 sts, 4 corner 2-ch sp).

Round 3: sl st into each of next 2 sts, sl st into corner sp, 3 ch, (2 dc, 2 ch, 3 dc) in same corner sp, 3 dc in next sp between 3-dc groups, *(3 dc, 2 ch, 3 dc) in next corner sp, 3 dc in next sp between 3-dc groups, rep from * twice more, sl st in top of beg 3-ch, fasten off (36 sts, 4 corner 2-ch sp).

Round 4: using yarn B, join with sl st to any corner sp, 3 ch, (2 dc, 2 ch, 3 dc) in same corner sp, (3 dc in next sp between 3-dc groups) to next corner, *(3 dc, 2 ch, 3 dc) into next corner sp, (3 dc in next sp between 3-dc groups) to next corner, rep from * twice more, sl st in top of beg 3-ch, fasten off (48 sts, 4 corner 2-ch sp).

Round 5: using yarn A, join with sl st to any corner sp, 3 ch, (1 dc, 2 ch, 2 dc) in same corner sp, 1 dc in each st to next corner, *(2 dc, 2 ch, 2 dc) into next corner sp, 1 dc in each st to next corner, rep from * to end, sl st in top of beg 3-ch, fasten off (64 sts, 4 corner 2-ch sp).

Rounds 6–7: as round 5; rep twice more, first using yarn B then using yarn A (96 sts, 4 corner 2-ch sp).

Rounds 8–11: using yarn B, rep round 5 four more times, but do not fasten off at end of each round; instead, sl st in next st, then sl st into corner sp to beg next round. Fasten off at end of round 11 (160 sts, 4 corner 2-ch sp).

Round 12: using yarn A, and with RS facing, join with sl st to any corner sp, 1 ch (does not count as st), *(1 sc, 2 ch, 1 sc) in corner sp, 1 sc in each st to next corner; rep from * to end, working a 16-ch loop if desired, in place of any corner 2-ch (see 'Hanging Loop', page 12).

Fasten off and weave in ends on WS.

CHRISTMAS TREE

Perfect for the festive season, this dishcloth features a bobble stitch Christmas tree motif for added texture. Rows of green bobbles decorate the tree shape, finished with a cheerful red bobble at the top. It's a fun, seasonal project that's both decorative and functional.

SIZE

Approximately 10in (25cm) square

YOU WILL NEED

- 1 x 93yd/85m/1¾oz/50g ball of 10-ply/ worsted (Aran) weight cotton in each of cream (A), brown (B), green (C) and red (D) (note that only oddments of yarn B and yarn D are needed). Shown in Scheepjes Cahlista 50g (85m) in Old Lace 130 (A), Chocolate 507 (B), Lime 512 (C) and Hot Red 115 (D)

- 4.5mm (UK 7, US 7) crochet hook

TENSION/GAUGE

Not critical, but as a guide, approximately 14 sts and 18 rows in pattern measure 4 x 4in (10 x 10cm) using Scheepjes Cahlista and 4.5mm (UK 7, US 7) hook

SPECIAL STITCHES

Bobble stitch (see page 12 for details)

INSTRUCTIONS

Using yarn A and 4.5mm hook, 34 ch.

Row 1 (RS): 1 sc in second ch from hook, 1 dc in each st to end, turn (33 sts).

Rows 2–4: 1 ch, 1 sc in each st to end, turn.

Rows 5–9: 1 ch, using yarn A, 13 sc, using yarn B, 7 sc, using yarn A, 13 sc, turn.

Row 10: using yarn A, 1 sc in each st to end, turn.

Rows 11–13: using yarn A, 1 ch, 5 sc, using yarn C, 23 sc, using yarn A, 5 sc, turn.

Row 14: using yarn A, 1 ch, 5 sc, using yarn C, (3 sc, 1 bobble) five times, 3 sc, using yarn A, 5 sc, turn.

Rows 15–16: using yarn A, 1 ch, 6 sc, using yarn C, 21 sc, using yarn A, 6 sc, turn.

Row 17: using yarn A, 1 ch, 7 sc, using yarn C, 19 sc, using yarn A, 7 sc, turn.

Row 18: using yarn A, 1 ch, 7 sc, using yarn C, (3 sc, 1 bobble) four times, 3 sc, using yarn A, 7 sc, turn.

Rows 19–20: using yarn A, 1 ch, 8 sc, using yarn C, 17 sc, using yarn A, 8 sc, turn.

Row 21: using yarn A, 1 ch, 9 sc, using yarn C, 15 sc, using yarn A, 9 sc, turn.

Row 22: using yarn A, 1 ch, 9 sc, using yarn C, (3 sc, 1 bobble) three times, 3 sc, using yarn A, 9 sc, turn.

Rows 23–24: using yarn A, 1 ch, 10 sc, using yarn C, 13 sc, using yarn A, 10 sc, turn.

Row 25: using yarn A, 1 ch, 11 sc, using yarn C, 11 sc, using yarn A, 11 sc, turn.

Row 26: using yarn A, 1 ch, 11 sc, using yarn C, (3 sc, 1 bobble) twice, 3 sc, using yarn A, 11 sc, turn.

Rows 27–28: using yarn A, 1 ch, 12 sc, using yarn C, 9 sc, using yarn A, 12 sc, turn.

Row 29: using yarn A, 1 ch, 13 sc, using yarn C, 7 sc, using yarn A, 13 sc, turn.

Row 30: using yarn A, 1 ch, 13 sc, using yarn C, 3 sc, 1 bobble, 3 sc, using yarn A, 13 sc, turn.

Rows 31–32: using yarn A, 1 ch, 14 sc, using yarn C, 5 sc, using yarn A, 14 sc, turn.

Rows 33–34: using yarn A, 1 ch, 15 sc, using yarn C, 3 sc, using yarn A, 15 sc, turn.

Rows 35–36: using yarn A, 1 ch, 16 sc, using yarn C, 1 sc, using yarn A, 16 sc, turn.

Row 37: using yarn A, 1 ch, 1 sc in each st to end, turn.

Row 38: using yarn A, 16 sc, using yarn D, 1 bobble, using yarn A, 16 sc, turn.

Rows 39–42: using yarn A, 1 sc in each st to end, turn.

Fasten off and weave in ends on WS.

EDGING

Round 1: using yarn C, and with RS facing, join with sl st to any corner sp, 1 ch (counts as sc), work 1 sc in each st and row-end around square (31 sts along each edge), and 3 sc in each corner. Join with sl st to first st (136 sts).

If desired, work a 16-ch loop (see 'Hanging Loop', page 12). Fasten off and weave in ends on WS.

TIP: When working the tree motif, use two separate balls of the main colour – one for each side of the tree. To help reduce tangling, wind off small balls for each colour block before you begin.

ROUND PADS

These small round pads are perfect for quick clean-ups or wiping down surfaces. Made in soft shades and a pop of fuchsia pink, they use a mix of bobble and cluster stitches to create a lightly textured surface that's both pretty and practical.

SIZE

Approximately 4¼in (10.5cm) across

YOU WILL NEED

- 1 x 27yd/25m/½oz/15g ball of 10-ply/worsted (Aran) weight cotton in three or four different colours of your choice. Shown in Scheepjes Cahlista 15g (25m) in Garden Rose 251 (A), Apricot 524 (B), Yellow Gold 208 (C) and English Tea 404 (D)
- 4.5mm (UK 7, US 7) crochet hook

TENSION/GAUGE

Not critical for this project

SPECIAL STITCHES

Puff stitch and 3 double crochet cluster (3dc-Cl) (see page 12 for details)

INSTRUCTIONS

Using yarn A, make a magic ring.

Round 1 (RS): 3 ch (counts as first dc), 15 dc into ring, pull yarn tail to close loop and sl st in top of beg 3-ch (16 sts).

Round 2: 1 ch (does not count as st), puff st in same st at base of 1-ch, *1 ch, puff st in next st, rep from * to end, 1 ch, sl st in top of first puff st (16 puff sts and 16 1-ch sp).

Round 3: sl st into next 1-ch sp, 1 ch (does not count as st), 3dc-Cl in same 1-ch sp, 2 ch, *3dc-Cl in next 1-ch sp, 2 ch, rep from * to end, sl st in top of first st (16 3dc-Cl, 16 2-ch sp).

Round 4: 3 ch (counts as dc), 3 dc in next 2-ch sp, *1 dc in next st, 3 dc in next 2-ch sp, rep from * to end, sl st in top of beg 3-ch (64 sts).

Fasten off and weave in ends on WS.

Make 3 more pads in yarns B, C and D.

BASKET WEAVE

With its woven look and thick texture, this basket weave dishcloth is ideal for both scrubbing and wiping. Finished with a neat moss stitch border, it's a stylish and practical addition to any kitchen, combining texture with a clean, modern finish.

SIZE

Approximately 9½in (24cm) square

YOU WILL NEED

▶ 1 x 185yd/170m/1¾oz/50g ball of sport/fingering (4-ply) weight cotton yarn in each of grey (A) and teal (B). Shown in Scheepjes Organicon Cotton 50g (170m) in Frosted Silver 203 (A) and Happy Thoughts 264 (B)

▶ 2.5mm (UK 12, US C/2) crochet hook

▶ 3.5mm (UK 9, US E/4) crochet hook

TENSION/GAUGE

Not critical, but as a guide, approximately 28 sts and 18 rows in pattern measure 4 x 4in (10 x 10cm) using Scheepjes Organicon and 2.5mm (UK 12, US C/2) hook

INSTRUCTIONS

Using yarn A and 2.5mm (UK 12, US C/2) hook, 55 ch.

Foundation row (RS): 1 hdc in second ch from hook, 1 hdc in each ch to end, turn (54 sts).

Row 1 (WS): 2 ch (counts as 1 hdc here and throughout), BPdc in next 4 sts, *FPdc in next 4 sts, BPdc in next 4 sts, rep from * to last st, 1 hdc in last st, turn.

Row 2 (RS): 2 ch, FPdc in next 4 sts, *BPdc in next 4 sts, FPdc in next 4 sts, rep from * to last st, 1 hdc in last st, turn.

Row 3 (WS): as row 1.

Rows 4–6: with RS now facing, rep rows 1–3.

Rows 7–33: repeat rows 1–6 four more times, then rep rows 1–3. Fasten off.

BORDER

Using yarn B and 3.5mm (UK 9, US E/4) hook, and with RS facing, join yarn with sl st to top right-hand corner stitch.

Round 1 (RS): 3 ch (counts as 1 sc and 2-ch sp), 1 sc in same corner, 1 ch, skip 1 st, *1 sc in next st, 1 ch, skip 1 st, rep from * to next corner, **(1 sc, 2 ch, 1 sc) in corner, 1 ch, skip 1 st, (1 sc in next st, 1 ch, skip 1 st) to next corner, rep from ** around, sl st in top of beg 3-ch, then sl st into corner 2-ch sp (52 sts along each edge and 4 corner 2-ch sp).

Rep round 1 three more times (58 sts along each edge and 4 corner 2-ch sp). If desired, work a 16-ch loop (see 'Hanging Loop', page 12).

Fasten off and weave in ends on WS.

ICE CREAM RIPPLE

Soft waves of gentle colour give this dishcloth a calm, classic look. The ripple pattern is easy to memorize once you get into the rhythm, creating a lovely textured fabric that's both practical and pretty. Worked in shades of vanilla and pale yellow it has a light, summery feel – a bit like scoops of ice cream in yarn form! It's an enjoyable make that's perfect for relaxing crochet time.

SIZE

Approximately 9½in (24cm) square

YOU WILL NEED

- 1 x 93yd/85m/1¾oz/50g ball of 10-ply/worsted (Aran) weight cotton in each of cream (A) and pale yellow (B). Shown in Scheepjes Cahlista 50g (85m) in Old Lace 130 (A) and Primrose 522 (B)
- 4mm (UK 8, US G/6) crochet hook

TENSION/GAUGE

Not critical, but as a guide, approximately 18 sts and 17 rows in pattern measure 4 x 4in (10 x 10cm) using Scheepjes Cahlista and 4mm (UK 8, US G/6) hook

INSTRUCTIONS

Using yarn A, 42 ch.

Row 1 (RS): 1 sc in second ch from hook, 1 sc in next ch, *1 hdc in next ch, 1 dc in next 3 ch, 1 hdc in next ch, 1 sc in next 3 ch, rep from * to end, working 2 sc only on last rep, turn (41 sts).

Row 2 (WS): 1 ch (does not count as st here and throughout), 1 sc in each st to end; change to yarn B on last yrh of last st, turn.

Row 3: using yarn B, 3 ch (counts as first dc), 1 dc in next st, *1 hdc in next st, 1 sc in next 3 sts, 1 hdc in next st, 1 dc in next 3 sts, rep from * to end, working 2 dc only on last rep, turn.

Row 4 (WS): as row 2; change to yarn A on last yrh of last st, turn.

Row 5: using yarn A, 1 ch, 1 sc in first st, 1 sc in next st, *1 hdc in next st, 1 dc in next 3 sts, 1 hdc in next st, 1 sc in next 3 sts, rep from * to end, working 2 sc only on last rep, turn.

Rows 2 to 5 set pattern. Rep rows 2–5 eight more times, then rep row 2.

Last row: using yarn B, 1 ch, 1 sc in each st to end, fasten off.

If desired, work a 16-ch loop (see 'Hanging Loop', page 12).

Turn dishcloth upside down to work along base of first row. Using yarn B, join with sl st to end stitch and rep last row.

Fasten off and weave in ends on WS.

TIP: To keep the edges neat on a ripple pattern, count your stitches carefully at the end of each row to make sure you haven't missed any. Stitch markers can be useful for marking the first and last stitch of each row.

CORNER GRANNY

This dishcloth starts with a classic granny square and grows with mitred rows along two edges, creating a striking angled shape. The bold combination of fuchsia, mustard and white gives it a fun, eye-catching look, and makes it a great stash-busting project.

SIZE

Approximately 9in (23cm) square

YOU WILL NEED

- 1 x 130yd/119m/1¾oz/50g ball of 8-ply/light worsted (DK) weight cotton yarn in each of fuchsia (A), mustard (B) and white (C). Shown in Scheepjes Catona Cotton 50g (125m) in Garden Rose 251 (A), Saffron 249 (B) and Snow White 106 (C)

- 3.5mm (UK 9, US E/4) crochet hook

TENSION/GAUGE

Not critical, but as a guide, 20 sts and 11 rows in dc measure approximately 4 x 4in (10 x 10cm) using Scheepjes Catona and 3.5mm (UK 9, US E/4) hook

PATTERN NOTES

The 2 ch at the beginning of a round does not count as a st, and you will crochet over it when the border is worked

INSTRUCTIONS

Using yarn A, make a magic ring.

Rounds 1–3: as rounds 1–3 of Green Granny Dishcloth (page 33); change to yarn B on last yrh of last st of round 3. Fasten off yarn A (36 sts, 4 corner 2-ch sp).

Round 4: using yarn B, as round 4 of Green Granny Dishcloth, fasten off (48 sts, 4 corner 2-ch sp).

Now work in rows along two sides of your granny square only, turning after each row.

Row 1 (RS): using yarn C, join with sl st to any corner sp, 3 ch (counts as 1 dc here and throughout), 1 dc in each st to next corner, (2 dc, 2 ch, 2 dc) into corner sp, 1 dc in each st to next corner, 1 dc in corner sp, turn (15 sts along each side and 1 2-ch corner sp).

Row 2 (WS): 3 ch, 1 dc in each st to corner sp, (2 dc, 2 ch, 2 dc) into corner sp, 1 dc in each st to end; change to yarn A on last yrh of last st, turn (17 sts along each side and 1 2-ch corner sp).

Rows 3-16: rep row 2 fourteen more times, working two rows each the following colour sequence: A, B, C, A, B, C, A (45 sts along each side and 1 2-ch corner sp).

Fasten off.

BORDER

Using yarn B, join with sl st to spare corner of granny square.

Round 1: 1 ch, 3 sc in same corner sp, 1 sc in each st around (approximately 45 sts along each side), working 3 sc in each corner, sl st in first st, sl st in next st. Work a 16-ch loop if desired (see 'Hanging Loop', page 12).

Fasten off and weave in ends on WS.

PUFF STITCH PADS

Made entirely of puff stitches and finished with a delicate scalloped edge, these small squares have a soft but firm texture. In a bright colour, they're both practical and pretty – perfect for gentle scrubbing, or for holding those warm pan lids in the kitchen.

SIZE

Approximately 4½in (11cm) square

YOU WILL NEED

- 1 x 137yd/125m/1¾oz/50g ball of sport/fingering (4-ply) weight cotton yarn in lime green (A). Shown in Scheepjes Catona Cotton 50g (125m) in Green Yellow 245 (A)

- 3.5mm (UK 9, US E/4) crochet hook

TENSION/GAUGE

Not critical, but as a guide, approximately 22 sts and 13 rows in pattern measure 4 x 4in (10 x 10cm) using Scheepjes Catona and 3.5mm (UK 9, US E/4) hook

SPECIAL STITCHES

Puff stitch (see page 12 for details)

SAFETY NOTE

These pads are not suitable for lifting pots and pans directly from a hot oven, but may come in handy for jobs such as holding warm utensils or lids.

INSTRUCTIONS

Using yarn A, 22 ch.

Row 1 (RS): 1 sc in second ch from hook, 1 sc in each remaining ch to end, turn (21 sts).

Row 2 (WS): 3 ch (counts as 1 hdc and 1 ch), skip next st, *puff st in next st, 1 ch, skip 1 st, rep from * eight more times, 1 hdc in last st, turn (9 puff sts, 10 1-ch sp, 2 hdc).

Row 3: 2 ch (counts as 1 hdc), *puff st in next 1-ch sp, 1 ch, skip 1 st, rep from * eight more times, puff st in next st, 1 hdc in last st, turn (10 puff sts, 9 1-ch sp, 2 hdc).

Rows 2 and 3 set pattern.

Rep rows 2 and 3 four more times, then rep row 2 once more. Do not fasten off.

BORDER

Round 1: continuing with yarn A, 1 ch, 1 sc in st at base of 1-ch, 1 sc in next 1-ch sp, *1 sc in each puff st and each 1-ch sp to last st, (1 sc, 2 ch, 1 sc) in last st, continue around square, working approximately 18 sc evenly along row-ends to next corner, (1 sc, 2 ch, 1 sc) in corner, rep from * once more, omitting final sc on last corner, sl st in first st (70 sts and 4 corner 2-ch sp).

Round 2: (2 ch, skip 1 st, 1 sc in next st) around, sl st in base of beg ch.

Fasten off and weave in ends on WS.

CAFÉ LATTE

This textured cloth is made with alternating single and double crochet stitches, creating a subtle but effective fabric for everyday cleaning. Worked in a soft light mocha with two darker brown stripes, it has a warm, coffee-inspired look. It's simple, stylish and perfect for kitchen use.

SIZE

Approximately 9¾in (24.5cm) square

YOU WILL NEED

- 1 x 137yd/125m/1¾oz/50g ball of sport/fingering (4-ply) weight cotton yarn in each of beige (A) and brown (B). Shown in Scheepjes Catona Cotton 50g (125m) in Camel 502 (A) and Hazelnut 503 (B)

- 3.5mm (UK 9, US E/4) crochet hook

TENSION/GAUGE

Not critical, but as a guide, approximately 17.5 sts and 18 rows in pattern measure 4 x 4in (10 x 10cm) using Scheepjes Catona and 3.5mm (UK 9, US E/4) hook

INSTRUCTIONS

Using yarn A, 43 ch.

Row 1 (RS): 1 sc in second ch from hook, 1 dc in next ch, *1 sc in next ch, 1 dc in next ch, rep from * to end, turn (42 sts).

Row 2: 1 ch (does not count as st here and throughout), *1 sc in next st, 1 dc in next st, rep from * to end, turn.

Row 2 sets pattern.

Rows 3–8: as row 2; rep six more times; change to yarn B on last yrh of last st.

Rows 9–12: using yarn B, as row 2; rep four times; change to yarn A on last yrh of last st.

Rows 13–32: using yarn A, as row 2; rep twenty times; change to yarn B on last yrh of last st.

Rows 33–36: using yarn B, as row 2; rep four times; change to yarn A on last yrh of last st.

Rows 37–44: using yarn A, as row 2; rep eight times. Do not fasten off.

BORDER

Continuing in yarn A, *2 ch, skip 1 st, sl st in next st, rep from * around, counting row ends as 1 st, then sl st in top of beg ch to join (86 sts, 85 1-ch sp). If desired, work a 16-ch loop to final corner (see 'Hanging Loop', page 12).

Fasten off and weave in ends on WS.

ZIG-ZAG STRIPES

This eye-catching dishcloth features a striking zig-zag pattern that adds a bright, modern touch to your kitchen essentials. Made in a playful mix of coral, pale blue, lime green, and mocha, it's a colourful and cheerful project that's as much fun to crochet as it is to use.

SIZE

Approximately 10in (25cm) square

YOU WILL NEED

▸ 1 x 93yd/85m/1¾oz/50g ball of 10-ply/worsted (Aran) weight cotton in each of coral (A), pale blue (B), lime green (C) and light brown (D). Shown in Scheepjes Cahlista 50g (85m) in Watermelon 252 (A), Baby Blue 509 (B), Green Yellow 245 (C), Camel 502 (D)

▸ 4.5mm (UK 7, US 7) crochet hook

TENSION/GAUGE

Not critical, but as a guide, approximately 14 sts and 18 rows in pattern measure 4 x 4in (10 x 10cm) using Scheepjes Cahlista and 4.5mm (UK 7, US 7) hook

INSTRUCTIONS

Using yarn A, 38 ch.

Row 1 (RS): 1 sc in second ch from hook, 1 sc in each ch to end, turn (37 sts).

Row 2: 1 ch (does not count as st), 1 sc in first st, *1 hdc in next st, 1 dc in next st, 3 tr in next st, 1 dc in next st, 1 hdc in next st, 1 sc in next st, rep from * to end; change to yarn B on last yrh of last st, turn (49 sts).

Rows 3–4: 1 ch (does not count as st), sc2tog, *1 sc in next 2 sts, 3 sc in next st, 1 sc in next 2 sts, sc3tog, rep from * to end, replacing last sc3tog with sc2tog; change to yarn C on last yrh of last sc2tog, turn (49 sts).

Row 5: 3 ch, skip st at base of 3 ch, 1 tr into next st (counts as tr2tog), *1 dc in next st, 1 hdc in next st, 1 sc in next st, 1 hdc in next st, 1 dc in next st, tr3tog, rep from * to end, replacing last tr3tog with tr2tog, turn (37 sts).

Row 6: 1 sc in each st; change to yarn D on last yrh of last st, turn.

Row 7: 1 ch, 1 sc in first st, *1 hdc in next st, 1 dc in next st, 3 tr in next st, 1 dc in next st, 1 hdc in next st, 1 sc in next st, rep from * to end, turn (49 sts).

Row 8: 1 sc in each st; change to yarn A on last yrh of last st, turn.

Rep rows 3–8 three more times, working 2 rows in each colour in the following sequence: A, B, C, D, A, B, C, D, A, then using yarn A, rep rows 3–7.

If desired, work a 16-ch loop (see 'Hanging Loop', page 12).

Fasten off and weave in ends on WS.

TIP: It's important that the peaks and troughs of the zig-zag pattern line up correctly, so count your stitches carefully as you work each row. Using stitch markers can also help keep your edges straight and the pattern balanced.

ALPINE STITCH

Alpine stitch creates a rich, textured fabric using front post double crochet, making this dishcloth ideal for tough scrubbing jobs. A bold block of deep teal forms the base, which is topped with fresh lime green, adding both visual contrast and a modern touch to this hardworking kitchen cloth.

SIZE

Approximately 9in (23cm) square

YOU WILL NEED

- 1 x 137yd/125m/1¾oz/50g ball of sport/fingering (4-ply) weight cotton yarn in each of teal (A) and lime green (B). Shown in Scheepjes Catona Cotton 50g (125m) in Dark Teal 401 (A) and Green Yellow 245 (B)

- 3.5mm (UK 9, US E/4) crochet hook

TENSION/GAUGE

Not critical, but as a guide, approximately 22 sts and 18 rows in pattern measure 4 x 4in (10 x 10cm) using Scheepjes Catona and 3.5mm (UK 9, US E/4) hook

INSTRUCTIONS

Using yarn A, 51 ch.

Row 1 (RS): 1 dc in fourth ch from hook (skipped 3 ch count as 1 dc), 1 dc in each ch to end, turn (49 sts).

Row 2: 1 ch (does not count as st), 1 sc in each st to end, turn.

Row 3: 3 ch (counts as 1 dc here and throughout), 1 dc in next st, *FPdc around post of next st (dc) from 2 rows below, 1 dc in next st, rep from * to last st, 1 dc in last st, turn.

Row 4: as row 2.

Row 5: 3 ch, *FPdc around post of next st (dc) from 2 rows below, 1 dc in next st, rep from * to end, turn.

Row 6: as row 2.

Rows 3–6 set 4-row pattern. Rep rows 3–6 four more times, then rep rows 3–5; change to yarn B on last yrh of last st.

Using yarn B, rep row 2, then rep rows 3–6 twice more, then rep row 3. Fasten off.

EDGING

Work for top and bottom edges.

Join matching yarn (A or B) with sl st to top right-hand corner st, 1 ch, 1 sc in same st, *1 ch, skip 1 st, 1 sc in next st, rep from * to end of row. If desired, work a 16-ch loop to top left-hand corner (see 'Hanging Loop', page 12). Fasten off.

Turn cloth upside down and repeat along opposite edge in matching yarn (A or B), omitting hanging loop.

Fasten off and weave in ends on WS.

POPCORN CIRCLE

This circular pad features a highly textured front made with popcorn stitches, perfect for scrubbing, paired with a double crochet back for balance. Finished with a neat edging and a handy hanging loop, it's a bright and cheerful accessory for those daily chores.

SIZE

Approximately 7in (18cm) across

YOU WILL NEED

- 1 x 27yd/25m/¼oz/10g ball of sport/fingering (4-ply) weight cotton yarn in each of: lilac (A), purple (B), pink (C), bright pink (D), light green (E), jade green (F) and bright yellow (G). Shown in Scheepjes Catona Cotton 10g (125m) in Lavender 520 (A), Ultra Violet 282 (B), Freesia 519 (C), Shocking Pink 114 (D), Tropic 253 (E), Jade 514 (F) and Yellow Gold 208 (G)

- 3mm (UK 11, US C/2) crochet hook

TENSION/GAUGE

Not critical, but as a guide, first 4 rounds of front measure 4in (10cm) across using Scheepjes Catona and 3mm (UK 11, US C/2) hook

SPECIAL STITCHES

Popcorn stitch (see page 12 for details)

INSTRUCTIONS

FRONT

Using yarn A, make a magic ring.

Round 1 (RS): 1 ch (does not count as st here and throughout), 8 sc into ring, sl st in first st to join (8 sts).

Round 2: 1 ch, *popcorn in next st, 1 ch, rep from * to end, sl st in first popcorn to join (8 sts, 8 1-ch sp).

Round 3: sl st in next ch sp, *(popcorn, 1 ch) twice in next ch sp, rep from * to end, sl st in first popcorn to join, fasten off (16 sts, 16 1-ch sp).

Round 4: using yarn B, join with sl st to any ch sp, starting in same ch sp, *(popcorn, 1 ch) twice in next ch sp, (popcorn, 1 ch) in next ch sp, rep from * to end, sl st in first popcorn to join, fasten off (24 sts, 24 1-ch sp).

Round 5: using yarn C, join with sl st to any ch sp, starting in same ch sp, *(popcorn, 1 ch) twice in next ch sp, (popcorn, 1 ch) in next 2 1-ch sp, rep from * to end, sl st in first popcorn to join, fasten off (32 sts, 32 1-ch sp).

Round 6: using yarn D, join with sl st to any ch sp, (popcorn, 1 ch) in every ch sp to end, sl st in first popcorn st to join, fasten off.

Round 7: using yarn E, join with sl st to any ch sp, starting in same ch sp, *(popcorn, 1 ch) twice in next ch sp, (popcorn, 1 ch) in next 3 1-ch sp, rep from * to end, sl st in first popcorn st to join, fasten off (40 sts, 40 1-ch sp).

Round 8: using yarn F, join with sl st to any ch sp, starting in same ch sp, *(popcorn, 1 ch) twice in next ch sp, (popcorn, 1 ch) in next 4 1-ch sp, rep from * to end, sl st in first popcorn st to join, fasten off (48 sts, 48 1-ch sp).

Round 9: using yarn G, join with sl st to any ch sp, starting in same ch sp, *3 sc in next ch sp, 2 sc in next ch sp, rep from * to end, sl st in first st to join, fasten off and weave in all ends on WS (120 sts).

BACK

Using yarn A, make a magic ring.

Round 1 (RS): 3 ch (counts as 1 dc here and throughout), 11 dc into ring, sl st in top of beg 3-ch to join (12 sts).

Round 2: 3 ch, 1 dc in same st, 2 dc in each st around, sl st in top of beg 3-ch (24 sts).

Round 3: 3 ch, 1 dc in same st, 1 dc in next st, *2 dc in next st, 1 dc in next st, rep from * around, sl st in top of beg 3-ch (36 sts).

Round 4: 3 ch, 1 dc in same st, 1 dc in next 2 sts, *2 dc in next st, 1 dc in next 2 sts, rep from * around, sl st in top of beg 3-ch, fasten off (48 sts).

Round 5: using yarn B, join with sl st to any st, 3 ch, 1 dc in same st, 1 dc in next 3 sts, *2 dc in next st, 1 dc in next 3 sts, rep from * around, sl st in top of beg 3-ch, fasten off (60 sts).

Rounds 3–5 set pattern of working 1 extra dc after each increase. Work five more rounds of increase pattern using colours C, D, E, G, G (120 sts) (see photograph above).

Fasten off and weave in all ends on WS.

MAKING UP

To join, hold front and back together, with RS facing out, join yarn G with sl st in any st through both sets of sts, (1 sc, 1 ch) in each st around (working through both sets of sts), sl st in first st, make a 16-ch loop (see 'Hanging Loop', page 12).

Fasten off and weave in ends on WS.

TIP: Popcorn stitch uses more yarn than basic stitches, making it the perfect stash buster. It also creates a lovely raised texture that's thick and sturdy, ideal for scrubbing.

SHELL STITCH

This delicate dishcloth showcases a beautiful shell stitch pattern, with several double crochet stitches worked into one stitch to create elegant, fan-like shells. Crocheted in soft lilac for a touch of sophistication, it's perfect for adding a subtle charm to your daily kitchen tasks.

SIZE

Approximately 9in (23cm) square

YOU WILL NEED

▸ 1 x 137yd/125m/1¾oz/50g ball of sport/fingering (4-ply) weight cotton yarn in lilac (A). Shown in Scheepjes Catona Cotton 50g (125m) in Lavender 520 (A)

▸ 3.5mm (UK 9, US E/4) crochet hook

TENSION/GAUGE

Not critical, but as a guide, approximately 3.5 shell sts and 13 rows in pattern measure 4 x 4in (10 x 10cm) using Scheepjes Catona and 3.5mm (UK 9, US E/4) hook

INSTRUCTIONS

Using yarn A, 50 ch.

Row 1 (RS): 1 sc in second ch from hook, *skip 2 ch, 5 dc in next ch, skip 2 ch, 1 sc in next ch, rep from * to end, turn (49 sts).

Row 2: 3 ch (counts as 1 dc here and throughout), 2 dc in same st, *skip next 2 dc, 1 sc in next st, skip 2 dc, 5 dc in next sc, rep from * to last 3 sts, skip 2 dc, 3 dc in last st, turn.

Row 3: 1 ch (does not count as st here and throughout), 1 sc in first st, *skip 2 dc, 5 dc in next sc, skip 2 dc, 1 sc in next st, rep from * to end, turn.

Rows 2–3 set pattern.

Rep rows 2–3 a further twelve times, or until your cloth is almost square, then rep row 2.

Final row (RS): 1 ch, 1 sc in each st to end. If desired, work a 16-ch loop (see 'Hanging Loop', page 12), fasten off.

BOTTOM EDGING

Turn cloth upside down and join yarn with sl st to top right-hand corner st, then rep final row once more, omitting hanging loop.

Fasten off and weave in ends on WS.

TIP: For a thicker, more durable dishcloth, try working the shell stitch in a heavier-weight cotton yarn. It still shows off the elegant shells beautifully while creating a sturdier fabric for everyday use.

LINEN STITCH

Worked in the round using linen stitch, this square dishcloth has a beautifully woven look with a neat, structured finish. The combination of deep burgundy and pale blue gives it a striking, modern feel, which is perfect for a trendy and functional kitchen cloth.

SIZE

Approximately 9½in (24cm) square

YOU WILL NEED

- 1 x 130yd/119m/1¾oz/50g ball of 8-ply/light worsted (DK) weight cotton yarn in each of pale blue (A) and burgundy (B). Shown in Nikkim Vinnis Colours 50g (119m) in Pale Blue-Green 518 (A) and Wine 580 (B)

- 4mm (UK 8, US G/6) crochet hook

TENSION/GAUGE

Not critical, but as a guide, first 11 rounds of pattern measure approximately 4 x 4in (10 x 10cm) using Vinnis Colours and 4mm (UK 8, US G/6) hook

INSTRUCTIONS

Using yarn A, make a magic ring.

Round 1 (RS): 1 ch, 1 sc in ring, *2 ch, 1 sc in ring, rep from * twice more, 2 ch, sl st in first st (4 sts, 4 2-ch sp).

Round 2: using yarn B, sl st into corner ch sp, 3 ch (counts as 1 sc and 2-ch sp), 1 sc in same ch sp, 1 ch, *(1 sc, 2 ch, 1 sc) in next 2-ch sp, 1 ch, rep from * twice more, sl st in first of beg 3-ch, change to yarn A and sl st in 2-ch sp (2 sc and one 1-ch sp along each side, four 2-ch sp).

Round 3: using yarn A, 3 ch (counts as 1 sc and 2-ch sp), 1 sc in same ch-sp, 1 ch, (1 sc, 1 ch) in next 1-ch sp, *(1 sc, 2 ch, 1 sc) in next 2-ch sp, 1 ch, (1 sc, 1 ch) in next 1-ch sp, rep from * twice more, sl st in first of beg 3-ch, change to yarn B and sl st in 2-ch sp (3 sc and 2 1-ch sp along each side, 4 2-ch sp).

Round 4: using yarn B, 3 ch (counts as 1 sc and 2-ch sp), 1 sc in same ch-sp, 1 ch, (1 sc, 1 ch) in each 1-ch sp to next corner, *(1 sc, 2 ch, 1 sc) in next 2-ch sp, 1 ch, (1 sc, 1 ch) in each 1-ch sp to next corner, rep from * twice more, sl st in first of beg 3-ch, change to yarn A and sl st in 2-ch sp (4 sc and 3 1-ch sp along each side, 4 2-ch sp).

Rep round 4 twenty-two more times, alternating between yarn A and yarn B on every round, ending with yarn B (26 sc and 25 1-ch sp along each side, four 2-ch sp).

On final round, if desired, add a 16-ch loop in place of a corner 2-ch sp (see 'Hanging Loop', page 12).

Fasten off and weave in ends on WS.

CRISS-CROSS

This dishcloth features a criss-cross stitch pattern with a subtle twist and open texture. With a navy-blue section in the middle, and light teal making up the rest, the colour splits highlight the stitch detail and add a cool, coastal feel to this practical and eye-catching design.

SIZE

Approximately 9in (23cm) square

YOU WILL NEED

- 1 x 130yd/119m/1¾oz/50g ball of 8-ply/light worsted (DK) weight cotton yarn in each of light teal (A) and navy blue (B). Shown in Nikkim Vinnis Colours 50g (119m) in Pale Blue-Green 518 (A) and Navy 589 (B)

- 4mm (UK 8, US G/6) crochet hook

TENSION/GAUGE

Not critical, but as a guide, 19 sts and 13 rows in pattern measure approximately 4 x 4in (10 x 10cm) using Vinnis Colours and 4mm (UK 8, US G/6) hook

INSTRUCTIONS

Using yarn A, 45 ch.

Row 1 (RS): 1 sc in second ch from hook, 1 sc in each ch to end, turn (44 sts).

Row 2: 3 ch (counts as 1 dc here and throughout), skip st at base of 3 ch, *skip next st, 1 dc in next 2 sts, 1 dc in skipped st (working across front of stitches just made), rep from * to last st, 1 dc in last st, turn (14 crossed sts, 2 dc).

Row 3: 1 ch (does not count as st here and throughout), 1 sc in each st to end, turn (44 sts).

Rows 2 and 3 set pattern.

Rows 4-11: rep rows 2 and 3 four more times; change to yarn B on last yrh of last st of row 11.

Rows 12-21: using yarn B, rep rows 2 and 3 five more times; change to yarn A on last yrh of last st of row 21.

Rows 22-31: using yarn A, rep rows 2 and 3 a further five times.

If desired, add a hanging loop (see 'Hanging Loop', page 12).

Fasten off and weave in ends on WS.

TIP: The crossed stitches give this pattern its distinctive texture. Make sure to work each stitch carefully and consistently, keeping the crosses aligned, so the pattern stays even and the fabric lies flat.

ACKNOWLEDGEMENTS

*Thank you, as always, to the wonderful team at Search Press for turning
my crochet dishcloth designs into such a beautiful book. And thank
you to everyone who loves to crochet as much as I do – you inspire me
every day, and I couldn't do it without you.*